W9-CYG-972

Freshwater Fishing

BY ALLAN MOREY

AMICUS HIGH INTEREST • AMICUS INK

Amicus High Interest and Amicus Ink are imprints of Amicus
P.O. Box 1329, Mankato, MN 56002
www.amicuspublishing.us

Library of Congress Cataloging-in-Publication Data
Morey, Allan, author.
Freshwater fishing / by Allan Morey.
     pages cm. – (Great outdoors)
Audience: K to grade 3.
Summary: "This photo-illustrated book for elementary students
describes the sport of freshwater fishing. Includes information on
safety and equipment needed, such as rods, bait, and tackle"–
Provided by publisher.
Includes index.
ISBN 978-1-60753-799-1 (library binding)
ISBN 978-1-68152-078-0 (pbk.)
ISBN 978-1-68151-019-4 (ebook)
1. Fishing–Juvenile literature. 2. Freshwater fishes–Juvenile
literature. I. Title.
SH445.M626 2017
799.1'1–dc23

                            2015023222

Editor: Wendy Dieker
Series Designer: Kathleen Petelinsek
Book Designer: Tracy Myers
Photo Researcher: Derek Brown

Photo Credits: Stockbyte/Exactostock-1491/Superstock
cover; Tatiana Bobkova/Shutterstock 5; IDAK/Shutterstock
6; Golden Pixels LLC/Shutterstock 9; John Kuczala/Getty
Images 10; Natasha Japp Photography/Getty Images 13;
MidwestWilderness/Getty Images 14; Stacy Love/Alamy 16-
17; Purestock/SuperStock/Corbis 18; Henry Georgi/Aurora
Photos/Corbis 21; Grigorev Mikhail/Shutterstock 22-23; Bill
Frymire/Masterfile/Corbis 25; Crisod/iStock 26-27; LWA/
Larry Williams/Blend Images/Corbis 29

Printed in the United States of America.

HC 10 9 8 7 6 5 4 3 2 1
PB 10 9 8 7 6 5 4 3 2 1

Table of Contents

Let's Go Fishing!

Imagine casting a fishing line into the water. You are watching a red-and-white bobber bounce up and down. Then suddenly it disappears beneath the waves. You got a bite! Your line goes tight. The tip of your fishing pole bends down. A fish tugs back as you crank on the **reel**. Does that sound exciting? Then you will enjoy fishing!

Got one! Fishing on the dock is a fun way to spend an afternoon.

Fish are not always caught to be eaten. A fisher sends this fish back into the water.

 Do people fish on the ocean?

Many people fish on freshwater lakes and rivers. Some catch fish to eat. Others do it for the thrill of hooking a big one. After catching a fish, they admire it. They may even take a photo. Then they let the fish go. This is called "catch and release." Someone else will have a chance to catch the fish later.

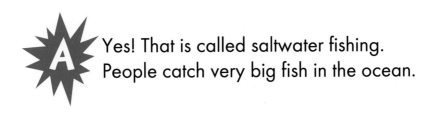
Yes! That is called saltwater fishing. People catch very big fish in the ocean.

What You Need to Fish

You can't fish without a fishing pole. Beginners should get a combo set. The rod, reel, and line will already be put together.

If you are just learning to throw your line into the water, or **cast**, try a **spin-casting reel**. It has a cover over the fishing line spool. A spinner inside helps keep the line from getting tangled up.

A combo rod and reel makes
learning to cast easier.

A fish chases anything that looks like food. Fishers put bait on their lines to catch fish.

 Can I use the worms I find in my backyard?

How do you attract fish? Bait! Live bait is the most common. People use different baits to catch different fish. For small **pan fish**, worms will do. For large bass, they use small fish called **minnows**.

Not everyone uses live bait. Some people use **lures**. Lures look like small fish or bugs. But they are made of metal or plastic.

 Yes, you can. You can also buy some at a bait shop.

A tackle box is also important. It carries all the other things needed to go fishing. Hooks hold the bait. They also hold fish onto the end of the line. **Sinkers** keep the bait underwater. Bobbers let fishers know when they have a bite. Pliers help fishers take hooks out of the fish they catch.

 Do you need anything special for big fish?

This small case holds a fisher's lures, sinkers, and hooks.

 Yes. A landing net will help you lift them out of the water.

**You will need a stringer
if you catch a keeper.**

 Do people need a license to fish?

Do you plan to keep the fish to eat? Then a **stringer** or a bucket is needed. After catching a "keeper," the fish is put on the stringer or in the bucket.

Also, a state fishing handbook is helpful. These books list the fish people are allowed to keep. States make rules about fishing. They want to make sure there are enough fish for everyone to catch.

 Maybe. In most states, anyone 16 and older does. Check your handbook.

For any outdoor activity, people need to be ready for the weather. Fishing is done mostly in open areas. Sunscreen and a hat are a must. You can get sunburned even on a cloudy day.

It can be cold and windy out on a lake. Fishers usually bring a warm sweatshirt or jacket. A poncho keeps them dry if it rains.

A hat with a wide brim helps protect from the sun.

Fish with a friend. It is safer. And
it will probably be more fun!

Safety First

Accidents happen. For outdoor adventures, remember this one rule. Always tell someone where you are going. It doesn't matter if it is a neighborhood pond or a secret fishing hole. If something happens, then people will know where to look for you.

Fishing is always more fun with someone. Grab a friend, and you'll be able to help keep each other safe.

When fishing, you will be around water. You might cast from shore or stand on a dock. These places can get slippery when wet. Pick your footwear carefully. Wear shoes with good **tread** on the soles.

If fishing in a boat, don't forget a life vest. It will help you float if you fall into the water.

 Can you fish in a canoe?

Life vests are always a good
idea. These fishers wear
their vests on shore too.

 Yes. Just be careful. Canoes can be tippy.

Fish have teeth. Some have really sharp teeth. They also have pointy fins. They flop around a lot after you catch them. On top of that, you are using sharp hooks to catch the fish. You may get some small cuts and scrapes. It is always good to have a **first aid kit** handy.

This pike has sharp teeth. Be careful!

Where to Go

If you haven't used a fishing pole before, start in your backyard. Put a sinker on the end of your line. Then practice casting. Once you are good at it, grab some bait. Then head to a local pond or river. Even lakes in big cities have fish to catch.

Some lakes have fishing docks. Cast a line into the water and see what you might catch.

Whether you are shore fishing or out on a boat, watch for good places to cast your line. Look for fallen trees or weed beds. Fish like to hide near these. Most fish swim in shallow water. Sometimes there are sandbars or sunken trees in the middle of a lake. These are also good places to fish.

Fish like to hide in underwater plants.

Have Fun!

Fishing can be exciting, especially if you hook a big one. It can also be rewarding. You may even catch a tasty meal.

Fishing is also about spending time with friends and family. You can share fish stories, even if the big one got away. But mostly, fishing is about having fun. Enjoy!

Freshwater fishing can be
a fun way to spend time
in the great outdoors.

Glossary

cast To throw the hook at the end of the fishing line into the water.

first aid kit Supplies such as band aids and antiseptic ointment used for medical emergencies.

lure A device that is used to attract and catch fish.

minnows Small fish used as bait.

pan fish A name for any small, freshwater fish, such a bluegills, perch, and crappies.

reel The part of a fishing pole that holds the fishing line; it often has a crank to wind the line onto the spool.

sinker A small weight that holds bait underwater.

spin-casting reel A reel that has a cover and mechanisms to keep the line on the spool and prevent tangling.

stringer A wire or rope used to hold fish.

tread The bumps and grooves on the sole of a shoe or boot.

Read More

Burlingame, Jeff. *How to Freshwater Fish Like a Pro.* Berkeley Heights, NJ: Speeding Star, an imprint of Enslow Publishers, Inc., 2015.

Carpenter, Tom. *Freshwater Fishing: Bass, Trout, Walleye, Catfish, and More.* Minneapolis: Lerner Publications, 2013.

Howard, Melanie A. *Freshwater Fishing for Kids.* North Mankato, Minn.: Capstone Press, 2013.

Websites

Fishing Facts | Freshwater Fishing Basics
www.fishingfacts.info/freshwater_fishing.htm

Freshwater Fishing Hall of Fame and Museum
www.freshwater-fishing.org/

Take Me Fishing | Freshwater Fishing
takemefishing.org/fishing/freshwater-fishing/what-is-freshwater-fishing

Index

About the Author

Some of Allan Morey's favorite memories from his childhood are camping every summer with his grandparents. While hiking, fishing, and camping with them, he grew to enjoy the outdoors. He still does those things, only now he takes his wife and kids with him.